The Language Codes

The Language Codes

R. Neville Johnston

SAMUEL WEISER, INC.

York Beach, Maine

First published in 2000 by
Samuel Weiser, Inc.
Box 612
York Beach, ME 03910
www.weiserbooks.com

Library of Congress Cataloging-in-Publication Data

Johnston, R. Neville.
    The language codes / R. Neville Johnston.
        p. cm.
    Includes index.
    ISBN 1-57863-144-0 (alk. paper)
    1. Self-actualization (Psychology)—Miscellanea.   2. Language
and languages—Miscellanea.   I. Title

    BF1045.S44 J64 2000
    131—dc21   99–089150

BJ

Typeset in 10.5/13 Carmina

Printed in the United States of America

07	06	05	04	03	02	01	00
8	7	6	5	4	3	2	1

Dedication

TO DEDICATE SOMETHING is to acknowledge gratitude. Gratitude is an attribute of satisfaction. What do you call someone who is never satisfied? An ingrate. One who suffers from an addictive mentality has lost gratitude, i.e., the ability to be satisfied. How might you retrieve the ability to be satisfied? A method would be by deprivation. Let's address food addiction. Fast for a week and I will guarantee that you will be grateful for whatever it is that you eat at the end of that fast! Furthermore, it will be very satisfying! Are you a shopaholic? Don't spend for a month. It will be satisfing. Whatever the addictive behavior, cut it off. Use the thought that Self-Love = Self-Discipline, and simply do it. Grace x Action = Gratisfaction (satisfaction or gratification). After the fast, or after deleting the behavior, you can reset. It is the very nature of rebirth. Here it is as math: If you are grateful for something, it is therefore satisfying. If you are satisfied, you are grateful: Satisfaction = Gratification.

If I were to dedicate this book to everything I am grateful for, there wouldn't be a tree left standing on this planet. I shall abridge the list: God, the Universe, my soul, my mind, my body, all my family, my father, my daughters Grace and Caramai, and their mother Ariane, all my friends, everyone who buys this book, everyone who suggests that others buy this book, everyone who attends my seminars, everyone who watches my TV show ("Telepathic TV, that's television that you watch with your Third Eye"), anyone who *never again* uses the word need, everyone who loves me and everyone I love, which is, of course everyone—for I have never met a human being I didn't find fascinating.

Contents

Preface

ONE WARM SPRING DAY (in 1977), I am with a beautiful actress. We are leaving the theater where we are thespians. Then suddenly—I am shot to death. A man, a total stranger, appears in front of us with a gun. He shoots me three times. I'll hear those shots for the rest of my life. The one that hits my head turns out to be fatal.

A few moments before this, I am feeling very good, looking forward to the next adventure the evening will hold. The night air is very warm and, pardon the pun, "muggy." As we approach the top of the steps of this literally underground theater, a man comes straight toward us, a chrome pistol in his hand.

Thinking it's a robbery, I begin to reach for my wallet. The next thing I know, I am looking at a hole in my new silk shirt. Looking at the wound, my brain is saying, "Look, that's the dermis, epidermis, yuck fatty layer, muscle. Wow, I have a muscle! That dark hole must be the inside of my stomach."

I look up to see what is happening. A second bullet hits my hip, and ricochets down into my left leg. It's still there today. Where is this coming from? As I look in the direction of the first two bullets, I see hairs from my head falling in front of my eyes. The bullet that impacted my cranium cut the follicles as it passed through the scalp/skull. I feel the warm gush of blood flooding down my forehead. I feel zero pain.

The man is running away. I am standing there watching him disappear into the crowd by the entrance to the theater. I look down to see a body lying there. It is wearing my clothes, lying in a puddle of blood, no eye movement. Humm . . . It's me!

I'm thinking to myself, "Gee, this is the best astral pro-jection that I've ever done. Ah, this may not be the best time to be astrally projecting; there may be some restriction on getting back into my body." I realize that an alarm bell is sounding. In fact, very loudly. Humm . . . That's my old high school fire drill alarm . . . Playing here? Upon my real-ization that it is justa "memory tape," the bell stops.

The next thought is, "Dust collects up." I never realized that dust collects on the ceiling. I know this because it's tickling my nose. During the entire experience my con-scious stream of thought never stops. The following thought is being in a room filled with white light.

I never experienced the tunnel that people talk about. The tunnel is an illusion that is created by looking at the light and then looking all around. I am just there.

Now because there is a brain between me and the white light, the light becomes an angel. Over the years I have done a lot of research into "near" death experiences (NDEs). The being who meets you, after death, has to do with your belief system. It could be Charon with the ferry across the river Styx, if you are a pagan. It could be Grandpa or an elder clan member if you worship ancestors in the Chinese or Native American traditions. Shamans who have passed over will take on the role of greeting in many tribal cultures. Whomever you meet, it is someone with whom you feel perfectly safe.

The being that is greeting me has the clearest blue eyes I've ever seen. Let's call him St. Peter. He is literally looking through a book, the book of my life, my file. I immediately begin the "Guilty Dance" saying, "I may not be doing the best possible job down there, given my talents and the cir-cumstances. Besides, I'm an only child and if my mother hears that I've been shot down this way it could kill her. Is there something that can be done?"

He says, "Chill." My angels speak to me in a sort of street vernacular. I immediately cease the guilty dance and am silent. A great calm comes over me. I feel very safe. He explains that the life I have just lived was just one more suit of clothes. It could easily be laid aside, meaning that this is just one more facet in my central soul—one more aspect of the wonderfulness of myself.

He says something that at the time totally exceeds my belief system. He says that those in heaven love many things about me. I could understand that "they" could like one thing, but love many things? I am amazed! What could they possibly love about me?

When the other soul shoots me, I forgive him on the spot. As the bullets enter my body, I am thinking, "If this person has a father, he is an abusive alcoholic." I cannot believe he has ever experienced being loved and certainly not as a child. I could only feel sorry for that other soul because he has chosen such a path.

I am remembering part of the lesson. I am remembering to forgive him, not to seek revenge, not to engage in the vendetta. I am wondering what else?

Next, in nanoseconds, St. Peter shows me fifty lifetimes where I have danced with this other soul. The first lifetime is set in a time period when humans are divided into clans. It is dark and wintry. We are in a cave warming by a central fire. Times are very hard, food wise. I am gnawing on some piece of cooked bird. My nemesis is pulling the food away from me. He just turns around and is walking away laughing.

I remember the smooth round stone, how it fits in my hand. I bean the little "dickens" right in the back of the head. He is dead before he hits the ground. He reincarnates. He kills me. I reincarnate. I kill him. Then he reincarnates and kills me, etc., etc.

The funny thing was that during the last four lifetimes, he kills me, I don't kill him. I said, "Pete, what is happening here? Gimmie me the skivvy. What, I'm four ahead? I get to knock him off four times, gratis?"

What is happening is that my hatred of him keeps this pattern in place. Therefore, I recreate him killing me those four times. The mnemonic is, *what you hate you recreate until you love it.* And believe me, I had more baggage stuck to me from those four lifetimes than a lot of others, because I judge him for killing me.

Therefore we were "stuck" to each other. What you judge sticks to you. Remember when you were a kid? I'm rubber and you're glue. What you say bounces off me and sticks to you. You may still be stuck to some of those kids. Unless you choose to forgive them. I don't mean forget them. I mean love them.

While all this is going on, I'm looking down next to me. I see a brook. I realize that there are souls in the brook, souls with whom I incarnate throughout time, my family of souls. I find that I can be a guest in other peoples' "soul streams."

They are all speaking at once. At first it sounds like babbling, but then I start to hear languages: Old English, Druid, some tonal languages I don't recognize. Again, because there is a brain between me and the sound, it translates into contemporary English. They are saying, "Give the kid a break, give the kid a break!" It is a magical sound, full of excitement, joy, and mystery. They are petitioning for a decision in favor of allowing my soul to return to this body.

"Peter," I say, "I truly love the soul that shot me to death. The work this soul does on my behalf is astounding. It's very labor intensive to knock somebody off fifty times. My path has included being a murder victim because I murdered in past lives. The moment he shoots me to death, he takes the burden off my shoulders and puts it on his. What a kind, noble, and loving thing to do."

He provides me with the "Shaman's Death," an initiation many of us choose at one point or another in life. I can clearly see the probable projection of this lifetime. It looks really good. I foresee even this moment of joy, as I sit here compiling this book. I adore this other soul. I love the bullet hole in my head. It acts like a radar dish. It is a tool of my shamanism. I complete the remembering with this other soul. I love this other soul. I love it all. To paraphrase the Borg, "love everything, resistance is futile."

St. Peter says that while he cannot let me go into heaven at this time, he could let me have a "preview." How wonderful! I take a step forward.

All my life, if you asked me, "Where does my soul live in my physical body?" I would say, "In my brain, the third eye."

When I step forward I expand, from the heart, not the head. Suddenly I am somehow an atmosphere around the planet. That is to say, I am everywhere on Earth at once. I am listening to perhaps a billion conversations at once. I can listen to any conversation I choose, especially if my name is in it. It seems all too confusing, all too new. I am very uncomfortable in this "new" form. This uneasiness is sensed.

The next thing I know I'm looking down at the top of a tree. There is a bird sunning itself. I think, "Gee, a feather. That's a solar energy collection device. A feather isn't 'hollow.' The energy goes in the flute, down the shaft and into the system of the bird. No wonder birds get up when the Sun comes up. No wonder they go to sleep when it goes down. No wonder they eat like birds. They're little, highly efficient, solar energy devices."

Come to think of it, as the energy enters the cortex of the bird, it experiences joy. Come to think of it, I'm the joy the bird is experiencing. The joy is love. The bird is experiencing love, being sunned. I'm the love the bird is experiencing. If you take anything and break it open, you'll find love inside and, come to think of it, I'm all that love!

Back in the reception hall, I'm told that I am a graduate. Because I remember to love the soul who shot me. The being I have danced with over the eons, I don't have to return to the body. Actually I feel disappointment.

Peter tells me that because of universal law he is required to inform me that, due to free will, I could go down there and blow it big-time. I tell him that I've paid my money and I want to continue the thrill ride called Planet Earth. Wow. . . . Do I own I volunteered to come here!

As he walks me to the door, St. Peter says, "Kid, glad to hear you wanna get back in the game. We're gonna give ya some marbles you've never had before." I'm looking at a door.

In the next scene my eyes are slowly opening. I am in a room . . . a hospital . . . IVs, monitors, the smell of disinfectant. I am feeling that same sense of calm. A nurse is walking by the foot of the bed. As she sees my eyes open, she makes a sharp right-angle turn in front of me. Instantly I see her in the civil war. She is a nurse. She is stunningly beautiful, even with blood splatters on her uniform. I can smell the gun powder; I can smell the blood. I can smell her. From the bed I see me as the broken Civil War solder floating above her head. The civil-war dimension of her looks up and begins to weep. I realize that I died in front of this soul-person in the Civil War. I come back to life in front of her in this life. *Fait accompli*, a loop tape closes in time. From this moment on, I have the ability to look into other peoples' multidimensionality.

As I explore my newly found abilities, I see a man, normal, in a business suit, crossing the street, swinging a cane. Interdimensionally, I see him in a monk's robe, followed by other monks. He is the one swinging the incense. I walk up to him and say, "You remember that village in Italy in 1358?"

He looks at me, pauses for a long moment and then slowly says, "Yes I think I may have a past life in that area." Then I say, "Yes, you do. Do you remember some of the people in your congregation?" Again the long, slow, "Yes." Then he asks what went on in this past life.

I tell him what I see in this brief moment. "You are such a beautiful man as you graduate the Vatican seminary. Your first assignment is to replace a priest who died after 66 years of service. You go to this village and slowly the people warm up to the 'new kid on the block.'

"Within two years it is the time of the Plague. There are so many funerals. Always you would end the service with, 'It's God's Will.' Relatives come to you and ask why God has taken this person. You only reply, 'It's God's will.' When 75 percent of the village is dead, the remaining 15 people come to your home. When you answer the door, someone hits you with a stone. You ask 'why' as they stone you to death. They keep saying, 'It's God's will."

This stranger looks at me and says, "Kid, you got a job." It reminds me so of Peter, it gives me a chill. The reason I am introduced to this man under these circumstances is to help him see who he is. He founded the Wisconsin Society for Psychic Research.

One day he calls me into his office and asks if I know why we have met this way. He says he has just realized that not once ever, in his entire lifetime, has he told people that they are the way they are because it is "God's Will." I work with this man for the next seven years.

Let's return to the present. I find myself writing a book. It will serve us well. The focus of this book puts us in a position to share the ownership of speaking a most powerful form of English—"Light-ease."

I used to call myself a teacher. I come from a family of teachers. Lately I'm thinking that a teacher is someone who bores us and then makes us wrong. These days, I prefer to think of myself as a storyteller. It's much more user friendly.

This book could have been written in flowery prose. Each remembering being could be presented in allegory. James Redfield mastered this form beautifully. Native Americans have owned it forever.

When I was in school, I would always get the Cliff Notes. They were most efficient. Then I could spend more time pursuing my truth—comic books. I believe we all have a great deal of reading to do so I'll just get right to the point. This book is in Cliff Note format. It is my opinion that this form serves us much better.

Barbara Hand Clow, in her book *The Pleiadian Agenda*,* mentions a particular home world. It orbits the star Maya. On this planet all education is in the form of games and storytelling. It is my ambition to see our Earth with such an educational system. There will then be only two titles in all of education—"Storyteller" and "Game Master." I love it! This book is a step toward that purpose.

The comic works in a profession that also owns language. Comedians play with words. In my earlier life I was a standup comedian. I observed that people only laugh when "it's true." Lately my motto is, "If you can't laugh at it, it's not healed." Great bumper sticker, eh? On to speak a language of clarity.

"We have already ascended"
Human consciousness has reached critical mass.

If you are reading these words, you have already ascended. That border has been moved behind us. Let's move on. What do we do now that we're ascended? Own that you are ascended. This book is focused on how to speak an ascended language, which will lead to even greater ascension.

As you read this book, you are in the future. Usually, past tense just separates us from an experience. An alternative is "we've ascended already." Perhaps, "we are ascension," is technically most accurate; however it's less understandable.

---

*Barbara Hand Clow, *The Pleiadian Agenda* (Santa Fe: Bear & Co., 1995).

Ascension has been promoted to the planetary level. Earth could not have done it without us. We could not have done it without her. [Both our species and our planet have done a very good job.] We are both doing a very good job.

Emancipation Proclamation

At the end of this book, you'll find your very own Emancipation Proclamation. Display it proudly if you choose. It is the "diploma" that rules all other diplomas. If you are wondering about who signs the proclamation, ask, "Who is the one person on Earth with enough authority to free me?" Think about it. Get the signature. Who is the only witness? God? Guess who God is.

The Manifestation of this Book

While in meditation, *I visualize the energy form of this book*—its wave form. It's the first form of its being. It glows in a pale iridescent green. It vibrates at an extremely high rate. The place that it's in is also made of a "magic substance." It rests on an altar. It is a Whole-y Book.

The book is more beautiful than I originally imagined. I connect the book to the publisher and the people who read it. Thank you for all the enlightenment it brings. Thank you, Angels, for your assistance.

I add light and intent to the book.

I ring the Crystal Bowls (tone it) to ground the vibration.

It comes down and grounds in 3-D.

It is so. I Love you . . . Read the book . . . It's really good. . . . And thanks!

Section I

Introduction

TO SPEAK THE CONSCIOUS LANGUAGE

THE POINT OF THIS BOOK—the reason you are reading this book—is to remember that we are living in the quantum field. In scientific terms, this means everything is vibrating. When you open your mouth and vibrate a word into existance, you program that field. That field is reality. The sounds you make in your language programs your reality! This book affords us an opportunity to do this consciously, instead of the way we have been doing it.

In the past few years there has been an enormous vocabulary increase in the light language. For example, just to know that you have a *frequency*, and that you are able to modulate it to receive different *channels*, enables you to do so.

Science has recently remembered that we live in a vibrational universe. Everything is vibrating. When we speak we are directing and focusing vibrations. Words have enormous power. They are a focus for our intent. The spoken word always manifests. Speaking the language creates a fluid of vibration. This fluid forms the reality of life to a larger extent than we may notice at first. Sound is a pure essence of the universe. We master the medium with our speech. Medicine, for example, is turning more and more to vibration as a set healing method. Since we are in a vibrating universe, the method of healing is vibration.

Ella Fitzgerald created, with her voice, a resonant wave, shattering that wine glass. The power of sound is more than just shattering a glass. Sound functions on etheric levels. Sound directed by thought in the form of words has great power. Words focus intent, the ethers, and reality. Words create reality.

In the movie "Dune," the hero was given his warrior name. When he spoke it out loud, it caused his weapon to fire. This is what we're talking about. Words manifest.

As our consciousness grows, it may become obvious that there were a few built-in flaws in spoken language. Our language had become the "Language of Lack." We had been tricked into using words that disempower. Just our luck, eh (joke)? The language itself was set up to express things in terms of lack, not abundance. Society itself is funded by and functions in the "Paradigm of Lack." Lack of money, lack of time, lack of love, had been our motivation. We had been driven by what appeared to be a lack.

We get out of bed, not because of money, but because of the lack of money. Every advertisement accuses us of not having something. The United States may be the richest country on the planet. How is it we are all so in debt?

This concept of lack leads to aggression every time. Every time we speak in terms of lack, lack is what we create.

Even to ask, "How are you?" implies lack. These days when someone asks me how I am, I reply, "Better and better, thank you." We program in lack, every day, with the power of words. When we change our speech, all life changes—both personally and planetarily.

One of—perhaps the greatest of all—the false paradigms introduced to this planet is the concept that everything we require is somehow outside of ourselves. We have to go out there and take what we "want." This concept will lead to war. The truth is that everything we require is already within us.

A guru in India is so kind as to agree to be buried alive for two weeks. When he is dug up, he doesn't even take a deep breath. He has been and is funding his existence directly from the universe. No food, no oxygen, no water, for that long. He reminds us that we already have LIFE within us. What we perceive as external is really within us.

The Hopi Indian language contains no way of expressing the concept for "the rock is over there." To speak that language is to realize that everything is totally connected. Everything is one. Everyone in our life is reflecting aspects of ourselves back to us. For example, there is a language in the Philippines that has no past tense. In fact, many "indigenous" languages have no past tense. A language in and of the now, how exciting! The majority of this text is written in present tense. The parts phrased in past tense are done that way to make it easier to comprehend.

Speech is powerful. The written word is powerful. Rhyming words activate the unconscious. Singing is powerful. Two voices singing together are power, a group singing and dancing together is most powerful.

In writing this book, it occurs to me that angels speak a language that doesn't include the concept of lack, that doesn't believe in anything but the abundance of God. Imagine that! Now speak it, now live it. I ask angels to assist me, and thank them all the time.

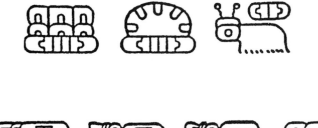

Section II

Negative Patterning

WORDS OF DISEMPOWERMENT

IN THE FIRST PART OF THIS book I would love to address some of the words of disempowerment that may still be in common usage. As you become *alert* to them and choose to discontinue their use, your everyday speech becomes a source of magnificent power.

Should

Whenever you say the word "should," you have made yourself or someone else wrong. The word "should" implies that a belief system has been violated. That belief system is guilt. Yes, you could have done something differently. So what? Everything always works out perfectly anyway. Why stew in guilt?

To quote Al Franken as "Stewart Smalley," the character from "Saturday Night Live," "There I go, shoulding all over myself again." Using "should" causes the ethers to become sticky and slow-moving. A much greater effort is required to get things to move, once you have decreed that something should be done. The word is inherently judgmental. *The difference between judgment and opinion is intent.* The intent of the word "should" is to make someone wrong!

At first, replace the word with "could." Realizing that you "could do something" rather than "should do something" is inherently freeing. It changes life from the obligatory to the voluntary. (After all, we all volunteered to come here, didn't we?) After some time, it becomes apparent that you are avoiding owning what you are saying by using even the word "could." You may begin to construct sentences around intent instead of supposition. It is more than two years since I have been aware of this concept and I still catch myself using "should." "Should" is a Middle Ages guilt-manipulation paradigm that doesn't work anymore!

Wait

As soon as you use "wait," you have put yourself or someone else on hold. How is this possible? Do you think of yourself as waiting on line, or waiting for a red light? These situations, in reality, are moments of *gratis meditation*. If you look at them, not as the halting of your will but as an opportunity to get a break from the maddening pace that had been impulsed into the human species, then life takes on a more relaxed air. Your timing becomes perfect.

It seems that the faster you want to go, the more stoplights you get. This is the universe responding to your opposition to the natural flow of the cosmos. This may be an irrational fear of a lack of time. All timing is perfect.

I first get this "waiting" for an elevator. The more impatient I become, the more time slows. When my watch actually stops, I realize that there is something that has not yet fallen into place. Why am I slowing down time so dramatically? Is it to allow myself to catch up? What have I not yet gotten? Why am I forcing this meditation on myself? The answer is to be calm; and when the word "calm" enters in my thinking, the elevator dings.

Whenever you perceive yourself as waiting, in reality your timing is being tweaked. These gratis moments of meditation correct your timing in life.

When you are feeling fulfilled, when you are enjoying life, being truly in the now, it is timeless. If you are judgmental, saying that "they" are not where they "should" be, not doing what they want to do, time takes forever. There really is no such thing as waiting. It's just a darker part of the illusion, the denial of self. *Life is an endless stream of access points to fulfillment.* Everything is an opportunity. There is a life worth living. Does carpe diem ring a bell?

But

When used in a sentence the word "but" takes back everything that preceded it. As in the infamous, "Yes, but," as in "I love you, but," . . . Well? Do you love me or don't you? This thought may be better phrased: I love you and when you behave in this manner, it upsets me, I choose that it evokes a fear in me. Then I attempt to make you wrong because I am dysfunctional; please forgive me. Then you are communicating. Then you are making no one wrong. If you say, "I would love to swim, but I'm afraid of the water," you are putting fear in the driver's seat.

You are constantly programming the reality of your life through speech and intent. If you have said something that you wish to take back, a proper term may be *cancel.* The word cancel does deprogram the ethers.

Karma

The concept of karma originally had a *quid pro quo* connotation, like a swing. For example, if you step on someone's foot now, in the next life he or she would step on your foot. I believe you have all noticed that getting your foot stepped on can repeat again and again. Where does it all end? Did I step on all those people's feet in past lives? Probably not. Fear of karma has been used to manipulate us into doing the right thing for the wrong reason.

The concept of karma has become a burden. Karma is, in fact, one of the Cosmic Laws. It is the Law of Cause and Effect. In this sense, karma and dharma are synonymous. We have all noticed patterns repeating themselves in our lives over and over again. We remember the lesson, then we forget it again. As soon as we remember who we really are, the karmic patterns are no longer necessary.

Rather than viewing ourselves as trapped on a wheel of karma, hopelessly in debt, treading forward through incarnation after incarnation, let's think of ourselves as in a position to recall that we are not just connected to the Divine, *we are Divine.* We can ask for angelic assistance in clearing the patterns in our life. If the angels, upon request, do clear a pattern, then we are in the position of remembering the lesson by grace. Don't forget to thank the angels, please.

The concept of karma is very old paradigm. Just agree to remember the lessons, effortlessly. The stepping-on-the-foot example is merely the courtesy lesson. Remember to say "Excuse me," and it all goes away. Otherwise, people will be stepping on our feet until the end of time, even though we may have initially only stepped on one foot. Say out loud, "I change effortlessly by Grace, thank you!"

Try

To try to do something is not to do it; it is to try to do it. The word presupposes failure. Werner Ehrhert founded EST behind this concept. To get "it" is to stop trying and start succeeding. Can't = Won't. Can't is a word spoken in the universe of excuse and blame, not in the user-friendly universe. For example: I won't fly through the air; I won't heal painlessly; or I won't change lead into gold. As soon as someone says he or she will *try* to be here, I "hear" he or she *won't* be here. Try to replace the word with attempt, endeavor, or intend (ha ha).

Need

The word "need" takes our power away every time. It robs us of our ability to create. Whenever we use the word "need," we identify a fear. The word "need" prevents us from having. To say that we need something means that we don't have it. It's a lie. If we pray, "Dear God, I need money," the prayer is instantly granted—we need money! We all have 100 percent of what we need. We have been programmed to ignore this fact. If we describe someone as needy, we have identified a very fearful person. "Want" is exactly the same in its effect. It is noted that all creation begins with a decision to have a desire.

We don't need love, we are love. We give love, we receive love, and we request love. Technically, we have no needs—period. "Need" may be replaced by "I choose," or desire or create—or most powerful—wish. We no longer "need" to ascend. The word "ascend" has become a barrier. As long as we need to do it, it won't happen. We are ascended. This is the only Ascension Manual you'll never "need."

Were we to replace the word "need" with the word "create"—Wow! Do it! If we stop using the word "need" our lives will instantly become less "needy."

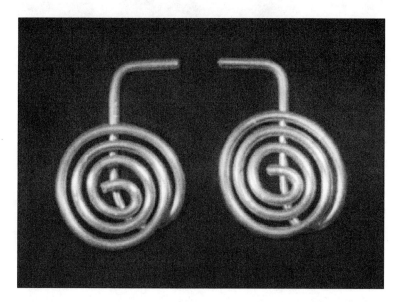

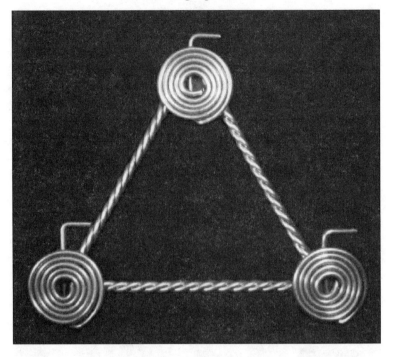

I Think

I think this one's obvious. Well, I guess so. No, it *is* obvious. The moment you use this phrase you give away your power to whomever you are talking with. Work with "I feel," or, "I know," or simply delete. "I think" really means you don't know. "I think" is a very disempowering term. What do you think?

Accident, Coincidence, and Mistake

These words do not exist. They may be replaced with the concept of synchronicity. If we look at the universe through a telescope, do we see anything "wrong?" Not possible. The universe, by definition, is perfect. Now look around on Earth. Where is the border past which things are right and wrong? There is no such border! For example, this book may contain what appears to be "typos." What, this treatise is the only thing in the universe that isn't perfect? Or are the typos a convenient excuse to invalidate the book, so one does not have to grow and change?

We are constantly programming our lives through the power of the words we use. It is time we speak in a way that better serves us.

Right or Wrong No Longer Exist
As soon as you make anything wrong, you are yourself wrong. Since it is inherent in the human mind to have choice, preference, taste, style, etc., you tend to have opinions. What you may say is, "a concept serves one or it doesn't serve one." Thinking in terms of right and wrong is inherently judgmental and it no longer serves us well.

Them and Us
There is no "them." There is only us. Sexism, racism, and patriotism are the worst of this dysfunctional paradigm. We could not even find a "them" on another planet. We are all connected. The military in that reality were the "Fashion Police." If someone wasn't wearing the correct uniform, he or she had to be shot. How stupid was that? To quote Christ, "What is there worth not loving?"

Guilt
Guilt is inherently about the past. This is always in a past in which you "should" have done something else. Well, so what! Yes, you could have done it differently, however everything works out for the best anyhow. So what were you worried about? Guilt destroys. You may recall "having loved and lost," and because of guilt, not remained friends with the person you love. Guilt destroys love. You have been genetically programmed for "guilt." You are no longer programmed in this fashion.

In my opinion, guilt is the main way to control others. It's not just mom and dad, it's everywhere. Are you guilty of any wrongdoing because you park your car? The parking ticket makes you guilty. It's your opinion you are not guilty. I suggest you own the concept, then and only then are parking tickets a thing of the past. *Guilt is the past tense of the word fear.*

Learn

We do not learn here on Earth, we remember. We came with all knowledge, we only have to remember. To discontinue the use of the word learn is to take the middleman out of education. Nothing is "learned" until it is remembered. There is only remembering.

Procrastination

You're probably putting off reading this one right now, aren't you? First, let me apologize for attempting to make you feel guilty about not reading this section because of my last comment. However, let's begin. We are given an assignment, or we set a goal. Almost immediately, we know how to go about accomplishing the task, but don't. Instead, we systematically list things that could go wrong, or don't start the project at all because we fear failure. What a waste of the human mind (just an opinion). Then all the time before the deadline gets eaten up. Moments before it's due, the project manifests as though by magic. I'm not saying it isn't "A" work, let's just examine the process.

One of the major procrastination submodems is to classify a project as "work." Therefore, the fear becomes, "I won't be enjoying life, if I begin." This is a major myth. May I suggest changing the word "work" to fulfillment, or exaltation of the creative process, or how about, play? Work = Play! What a thought! Then the sentence becomes, "When I play the assignment game, I am having fun and getting fulfilled at the same time." There is no reason why life would not be enjoyed with the project underway. In fact, life becomes more enjoyable once you have begun, because the deadline is no longer such a threat.

As the saying goes, "What goes wrong is always something that we didn't think about." So why bother to think about what could go wrong? Actually start your project, and if something does go wrong, *then and only then,* deal with it. Thinking about what might go wrong brings possible negative futures to the project. Being in this negative future paralyzes the present and nothing gets done. We can all agree that thought creates, so why would we create a negative future for someone we love—namely ourselves?

Let's take a look at it in more simple terms. Back in school, you are given a weekend home"work" assignment. Is the weekend time off, yes or no? I'm a 7-year old and the system is already turning me into a procrastinating workaholic. How about home-play, no longer homework!

Here is how it works. The assignment is put off on Friday, but you think about it. Saturday, also, but you continue to think about it. Sunday night or even Monday morning you do the work. The work is finally started because of guilt, not desire. This simply doesn't serve you very well. What percent of the weekend was yours? The assignment took all weekend, however you only worked a few hours. How is this possible?

The only way out is to arbitrarily break the cycle. Do the assignment when you get it. As a "deadline addict," you became dependent on this external structure to get anything accomplished. Arbitrarily do the work long before the deadline. Then create a week off. What do you do? You have never had time off before. Probably sleep! Sleep was robbed out of the cycle every time (the famous "all-niter").

As a procrastinator, life is built into a tidal wave of deadlines. The next one is always approaching. You are always on, always running late. There is no peace, no downstroke in the cycle, no boredom. This downstroke is essential to the creative process.

We give you that if necessity is the Mother of Invention, boredom is the Father. The Wright Brothers are an example. They were bicycle mechanics. They must have been bored to tears. Finally, one said, "I'd like to build a bicycle that can fly!" Every tool in the house got used. Modern aviation was created more through boredom than necessity. Boredom, the downstroke, is necessary; once we have created it, it becomes quintessential. Heretofore we have been "running on batteries" without much recharging. Once the break is created, it becomes indispensable.

In order to help with the reprogramming, I would like to coin the term "Thought Efficiency Quotient." This is an index of the number of thoughts necessary to accomplish a goal. For example, if you decide to pick up an object, but don't do it, your thought efficiency quotient is already divided by two. You have to start from scratch, thinking the exact same thought again. "Pick up the object." If you think of it again, and again don't do it, your thought efficiency quotient is divided by the number of times you think about it. These "wasted" thoughts over a lifetime add up to an enormous percent of the lifetime.

The essence of procrastination is the fear of commitment—not to the project, but to a *fear of commitment to yourself!* Nothing can happen until there is commitment; this is the true block. We have been programmed to doubt, especially ourselves. We are made afraid to commit, because something could go wrong. Again, so what?

In procrastination, the two separate processes of planning and doing have become muddled. Planning is the female energy and doing is the male energy. The procrastinator may continue the planning process long after the doing end of things has been completed. He or she may still be thinking of possible processes years after the job is completed. I wish to delineate a clear border between the two processes. A clarification of the on/off switch is requested. When I switch from planning to doing, I switch off planning. That's all there is to it. This switch is a gift, I am free to accept it effortlessly.

Not that I mean to quote a popular tennis shoe company, but if you want a simple cure for procrastination, that would be, "Just do it!" Oh, just one more mnemonic: self-love is self-discipline. So many of us are not afraid to die. We are afraid to live. Choose this moment, now commit to life.

Falling in Love

Please . . . When you become in love, you ascend, you don't fall. Talk about the language being 180 degrees from the truth! Have you noticed that being in love ups your frequency? Another thing I adore is changing the standard greeting from "hello" to "You are my beloved," or "I open my heart to you." Practice it a few times and enjoy. Every relationship started in this manner is automatically on a higher frequency.

Anger = Missing Information

Have you ever noticed you can be very angry, then someone walks into the room and speaks one sentence, and all the dark clouds vanish instantly? Anger always equals missing information. As anger builds, before the brain chemistry becomes unbalanced toward acidic, quiet the mind and ask for the missing information. It will be given. You will feel or hear it. You now have the faith for the knowing of this information.

Anger means that your attention is requested on a particular issue. Just focus; to explode is totally unnecessary. One of the things to love about anger is that it is a cue. It's the point at which you do something about a situation. It signals the time for change.

Anger = Fear

What are you so frightened of that you are choosing anger? Fear is the root of anger. In this way you deal with the fear instead of cleaning up after the anger.

Anger, unhealed, turns into addictive behavior. Addiction = Anesthesia. Addiction is the harmony lesson. You "know" that you require the substance of addiction to be in harmony. Nonsense! There is one and only one thing in this universe that could create a person out of harmony. That is yourself. This is why people have problems with addictive behavior.

Hatred is a Mirror.

We see in the mirror of hatred a part of ourselves. This part is the part that we do not like or love about ourselves. The other person we are looking at is reflecting back some part of ourselves that we don't like.

That was actually very kind of the person involved. We may wish to thank that other person for having that trait, because then we don't have to have the characteristic ourselves.

The example of someone cutting in front of us in traffic: Oh, we hate that person! We fall asleep that night thinking of mashing his or her molecules. This becomes a loop tape that can take up hours and a great deal of life-force. Besides, if we really hate being cut off in traffic, it is likely we will recreate it.

Consider that we hate the driver for not paying attention, yet it is really ourselves that weren't paying attention. We wish to thank the person who cut us off for awakening us. Believe it. We are awake after being cut off. Besides, the other driver gave us an adrenaline rush equivalent to sky diving!

Now, because we hate this person for their discourtesy —what? We race through traffic to catch up to that rude person to flip that person a single-digit salute? These days consider flipping them the peace sign. We will be saying: "We're not going to go to war with you over this. If you want to go to war, you'll have to do all the work." That'll really piss 'em off. Mnemonic: *What we hate, we recreate, until we love it.*

Aggression = The Mentality of Lack
Rather than the Mentality of Abundance

Whenever you exhibit aggression, it is because you are functioning in lack. This causes others to resist. Aggressive behavior casts everyone around you in an adversarial role. This may not serve you very well. As the species becomes fully awake, it is no longer necessary even to "ask." There is no lack! Others' lovingness toward you and yours back to others has always been here; just now it's normal.

Fraud

Herd mentality is part of us ALL. Now, in herd mentality, all of this "new-fangled" consciousness stuff is not real. Therefore, some part of you believes that you are fraudulent. This makes it somewhat impossible to make money if you have choosen to be "Light-Workers." Actually, it's "Light-Players."

Personally, your author wrote the following affirmation:

> It is safe for me to no longer perceive my self as fraudulent. I am no longer fraudulent. I own that I am not fraudulent. I am genuine.

A Life of Fearlessness

Which is easier? Check one.

☐ A life of Fear
☐ A life of Fearlessness

If you checked a life of fear, it perfectly illustrates just how programmed, trained, impulsed, and genetically engineered you have been to fear the unknown. Yet you are always so curious. It is your nature to explore.

You now see what a perfect short circuit has been installed in your former way of thinking. "Unknown =

Evil." This safeguard was designed to make it difficult for people to awaken. You can just dance that one right off. You have all lived the life of fear. If for no other reason than variety, consider checking fearlessness.

A Developed Immune System to Fear

Picture a beautiful forest. Trees and wildlife overlook a breathtaking vista. You feel safe, empowered, alive! Now, picture an urban environment—sirens, angry people, concrete under the feet, etc. There is a profound difference. That difference is the presence of fear. It is the true form of pollution. Thought forms, for example, form along roadways where there are commuters all thinking the same negative thoughts at the same time, every day, during rush hour.

In the forest, the trees conduct the negative energy effortlessly back into Mother Earth. If you leave a car battery just on the earth itself, it will not drain. If you sit it on a slab of concrete, it will drain rapidly.

Sprawling cities cover the Earth with fifty square miles of concrete. The fear vibration collects and intensifies. Fear is only programming. It's not really a natural state. It exists outside the self, and therefore you may appear to be subject to infection from it.

It used to be that all people led a life of fear. They made a surprisingly large number of life's decisions based on what could go wrong. Then we remembered Fear = Fiction. *All fear is the same thing.* First, understand how fear works. The object is to remember how to recognize a fear-thought. Every fear is actually *the same thought. They all create us in a dark future. We're not actually in that future. We just think we are. Our lifeforce drains just as though we are. Fear is anything that makes us feel bad.*

The trick is to recognize that we're in a dark future and to pull ourselves back to the present. A dark thought in the past is called guilt. Guilt is the past tense of the word fear. Guilt always takes place in the past. It is where we are tortured by what we could have done. It all worked out perfectly anyhow. Fear is always the same. What we're afraid of isn't actually happening, we are just thinking about it happening.

Fear-thoughts Always Drain Our Lifeforce

Good news, we have a gift for you. It's called THE OFF SWITCH FOR FEAR. Seven years ago, I assigned a bunch of brain cells to perform one and only one function. They were to alert me that I was having a fear-thought. They would trigger and I would remember to come back to the now. It so happened that after triggering about ten times in a row, I'd leave the now just as quickly and go into fear. I had to shut down, go to sleep. I thought my brain was broken. It appeared that it could only generate fear-thoughts. What a lie!

The times when I am fearless are growing longer. Those relapse panic attacks, sadnesses, depressions, etc., are far less in duration, they have disappeared completely.

As soon as you realize you are having a fear-thought, Shut It Off! To better understand fear is to understand that there is only one fear-thought. It's called the BIG LIE. Every lie you've ever told, every lie you have ever heard, is based on the Big Lie.

Fear is always based on a profound feeling of our own inadequacy. We humans have for a very long time been functioning with the false premise that there is something wrong with each and every one of us. A part of each of us is somehow missing. What? We were absent in school one day? We can never retrieve that missing piece? The Big Lie is, "I am inadequate."

In the next sentence, I will prove this is a lie. Ready? You have always dealt with anything you created for yourself. You are not now, and never have been, inadequate, period. You've dealt with it all! This lie rules us—no longer by our choice.

"I am inadequate," is a corruption of the code that is each person's private access to the Godhead. The true sentence, the "Big Truth," is simply, "I AM," or "I AM that I Am."

Fear isn't actually happening: People on this planet are raised to be extremely fearful. Fear is addiction, itself. We have become addicted to fear. Choosing to boldly move forward into the life of fearlessness equals overhauling the entire way we have been taught to think. Lord, it is fun.

Why we have been raised to be fearful: Throughout this book we have been talking about how thoughts manifest. Ever notice fear-thoughts don't manifest that much? Where does the energy go? It is our personal lifeforce, that fear. What happens to it?

Actually, it is food. Food for other-dimensional beings who are dark. They don't require the human race as their food. They just don't realize it. Blessings upon them.

We weren't just accidentally raised this fearful. It has been well planned. We have been genetically engineered for tears, depression, anger, etc. Our species is being up-graded-from two DNA helixes to 12. Just ask, and it is done.

Ladies and gentlemen, we were food. Our fear-thoughts used to feed some nasty stuff. We stopped feeding them, they went away. Wean the self off the addiction called fear. Besides, *fear is boring.*

Are Control Freaks Annoying the Feces out of You?

What is the one and only thing that can control you? Answer: You! Let me ask the same question in another way: What percentage of your life do you create? When you answer 100 percent, congratulations are in order. You are a "descended" Master.

Bullies. Aren't they fun? Have you ever seen a bully attack someone? Bullies get more than lunch money, they get our *manna* (our life force). The first thing bullies do is make someone wrong. Next you are expected to act guilty. Then, through the process of your own stewing, they suck all available life force from you if you have chosen to play the role of victim. Then you choose to let others "control" you. Actually you are still controlling yourself. The bully principal works only with your total cooperation.

It's not so much about being beaten up, it's the hours of going over it in the mind, the same loop tape again and again. Boring isn't it? What can you do about it? How do you stop the cooperation? How do you get it to go away? How do you love it?

To enter higher-dimensional consciousness is to triangulate, to depolarize (i.e., balance, for example, the concepts of right and wrong). The process involves seeing it from above, as though looking down at an enormous yin yang symbol. Then everything is perfectly in its place, all making the joy of wholeness. In this light, something isn't right or wrong; it simply is.

We all have our individual truth. This study of our bipolar universe may be more effective if the two poles are considered to be love and fear. This applies to all the terminology with which we are familiar—them-us, male-female, good-bad, etc. The human race constantly vibrates between these two opposites. First we love, then we hate (and destroy), then we love again (and rebuild). The example of the relationship with our parents over a lifetime may illustrate this concept perfectly.

Once we as a species remember the secret that *the master always knows that everything has already come out right*, evolutionary acceleration takes place! Once we remember the secret that everything is worked out perfectly in the now, we live in Heaven on Earth.

How can we operate in wholeness? We are all allowed to be where we are on our individual learning curve. Especially ourselves. We are all perfect exactly the way we are. Now we can think much more freely. Now we are in a position to deal with people without making them wrong.

All controllers are operating from their own fear. Their fear is about their own inability to control themselves. Here is where compassion lies.

A key to understanding the cure, the resolution for the *external control battle*, is in the realization that it is actually an *internal control battle*, perfectly externalized as our life. Anything we see through our senses right now is an aspect of ourself. Without exception. The brilliance in this treatise is our brilliance. Conversely, things that we don't like to look at are the parts of ourselves we don't like to look at. *The only control that there is in the universe is internal control (self-control).* Those studying Zen have it perfectly phrased in *Esho Funi.* Inside = Outside.

It may be fruitless to attempt to change anything in our external world, because it will only perfectly reflect the internal world. Therefore, the only work that can be done is work on ourselves, on our insides. As the country-and-western song says, "Wherever you go, there you are."

Whenever any issue comes up, whenever you "bite at the bait," you become entangled in external nonsense. The concept is to first examine your internal structure to discover the true nature of the conflict you have been offered. As this unfolds in your thinking, it is obvious that no one is wrong. You are then in a position to thank those who play the role of bully, for they have assisted you to see what's going on inside.

> When you function in love,
> your inside creates your outside.
> When you function in fear,
> your outside creates your inside.*
>
> —Drunvalo Melchizedek

All of these concepts have been perfectly illustrated in a Star Trek episode in which Worf (the Klingon) and his girl-

---

*Drunvalo Melchizedek, in a presentation at the Earth Sky Workshop in Baltimore, MD on December 13, 1997.

friend, Jadzea Dax, were to go on vacation to the pleasure planet. Worf was very grumpy and made everyone on the planet wrong for having fun. He went so far as to take the weather grid off-line, causing it to literally rain on everyone's parade. Actually, Worf's true fear was that if he did enjoy himself, even a little bit, he would lose control of himself. Then, no one would be safe. He externalized it perfectly. Others found it difficult to play with him.

All Fear is the Fear of Separation

Emotions equal energy in motion. Fear and emotion are two quite different things, even though they are both energy in motion. Sadness, anger, depression, loneliness, hatred, greed, envy, lust, and frustration are fear emotions. This means that they are not really emotions, because they are simply fear, and all fear is the same thing. All fear is that you may somehow be inadequate.

Sadness is the fear that others will not understand what you have been through. Depression is the fear that you will change. Loneliness is the fear of separation. How is it possible to be alone when you always have yourself, guides, and angels, etc.? Greed is the fear that you will never get enough. Envy is the fear of imbalance, that someone has more than you do. Lust is a combination of all of them sent through a sexual pulse. Frustration, being in a rush, and laziness are a fear of time. Any embarrassment is the fear that others will (won't) recognize your truth. Confusion is the fear of failure. Apathy is the fear that if you care, you will become vulnerable and therefore hurt.

In order to experience love, you must be willing to risk pain. In participating in love, you live. Ladies and gentlemen, place your bets! In participating in fear, you die.

Emotion—yes! How about love, joy, happiness, inspiration, adoration—can you feel your emotional body healed? Say yes out loud, say it just like the Pentecostal Priest—Yes, YES! Y-E-S!!! Oh Lord, Yes!!!!

Fearlessness the Chart

- We train our minds to recognize the fear-thought I am inadequate. (I won't be able to deal with it.)

- Fear is *any* thought that makes us feel badly. Our bodies easily recognize fear. Fear has more than trillions of disguises.

- The moment fear is recognized it is dismissed. Your life-force is returned to you.

- Fearlessness does not equal stupidity. We have stated that fear had many disguises.

- Fear is boring.

Wife, Husband, Marriage—All = Death/Slavery

We have all had so many past lives that these words—wife, husband, marriage—have come to be associated with the greatest of frustration—confusion and lack of fulfillment. If I am husband or wife I am enslaved until I die. This is the "herd mentality" paradigm, and it is a myth.

Children have brought with them some of the greatest models of behavior available. Children on the playground agree that they will be companions (i.e., playmates). This agreement is set up for no particular length of time. When it is over they both know it. From this moment on, our friends may be referred to as our playmates until another choice is made.

The way it had been: you find 'em, you like 'em, you love 'em, you get rid of 'em. Until the awakening, this is 100 percent of adult romantic relationships. The other starts to get close. You feel unsafe, enslaved, so you push the person you love away.

To dissolve this myth, allow me to ask: What is the one and only thing that controls you? Okay, let's say we're in the military and I order you to execute someone. Who does the executing? The answer is that you are the only thing that controls you. It is not God, free will, after all. You are the only thing that controls you. Can your spouse control you? Of course not. Please own this.

Hello, My Name is Neville and I'm
a Recovering Doubtaholic, I Think (pause for laugh)
I know I'm a doubtaholic no more. I have survived being a doubtaholic. Now I survive not being a doubtaholic. It is safe to no longer be a doubtaholic.

I don't doubt.

Well, sometimes.

Ahh . . . doubt is a discernment remembrance.

It's situational, specific, it just depends.

Doubt used to be a barrier.

Doubt is no longer a barrier.

Sugar

My life is quite sweet, thank you. I have no need of dietary supplements.

Years ago, on the very first "Deep Space Nine" episode, there was a character named Tausk. He was offered a ride in the Holosuite. His reply was, "Fantasy? I have no need of fantasy. My life is already the greatest adventure imaginable!" Wow! I spend 48 hours in the fetal position, whining that my life isn't the greatest adventure imaginable. Then I realize that this whole concept is simply a decision. I make it.

Sometime later, I return from a "near" death experience. I assign a new guide. This being appears to be an orangutan.

At this time, it was my body that decided on a five-day fast. A friend and I had produced four one-hour specials for TV. We went out to dinner. Both my body and I decided to end the fast. We went to a delightful African restaurant. At the end of dinner, coffee was served and I reached across the table for the sugar. I felt this guide's hand on my arm. He said, "My life is quite sweet. I have no need of dietary supplements. Thank you."

This guide turned out to be Thoth. He does appear as an orangutan. Since then, I see people in bakeries and wonder how to remind them of how sweet their lives are. As I have stopped using processed sugar, I notice I use the word sweet to describe many of life's situations or people. My life is quite sweet. We used to have a tendency to accept substitutes for love in our lives. The sugar cartels had stolen the sweetness from our lives. Love—accept no substitutes.

The Real World—The Definition of Sanity

Many of us who agree to follow the path of light do so in our "spare" time, then we go to a "real" job. This use of language makes light not so real. Live in the world of light at all times. Please. In the old paradigm, sanity was defined by living a life we hate, doing things we detest in order to support ourselves and our families. Pardon me, get real! Does a dysfunctional family(life) in material splendor really begin to equal sanity? The definition of sanity is happiness. Sanity = Love. Insanity = Fear.

Sorry

To say you are sorry is the denial of your own essence. Apology is sometimes essential to the healing. You may say that you may not have served yourself or others very well by a certain act, however it is my opinion we have all done "sorry" to death (i.e., our death).

The Comparison Game

If you play the comparison game, you automatically lose. Let's use the example of your author comparing himself to Deepak Chopra. Automatic loss! The light of your author may appear to be the lesser of the two. Nope! We are all brilliant lights. Deepak may serve as a wonderful model, however, your author is no less brilliant. I would not choose to change places with Deepak, because I would miss the wondrous opportunity to be me!

Apples and oranges, each is brilliant, each serves very well. The one you choose is based on mood. This is the way it is in every comparison you make. Neither one or the other is "better," just different. In the old comparison game, one is right, one is wrong. It doesn't work that way. You may prefer one, and that's it. There is a win-win outcome for everything. Identifying the win-win = universal backup.

For Our Highest Good

Since our involvement in consciousness acceleration, everyone and his uncle has said that the reality we experience is created (and approved of) by our higher selves.

I have a dramatically different opinion. *It is our uncon-scious mind that creates the realities of life, not the soul.* To reach the higher realms, we first go through the lower realms. The unconscious mind has been so poorly pro-grammed that these little *faux pas* appear to keep getting in the way. The higher self approves of this so that we can catch on to the desirability of reprogramming our uncon-scious mind. For example, the higher self approves of play-ing the role of victim again and again until we remember unconsciously that there are no victims!

Germs Don't Make You Sick—You Make You Sick

There are three methods we use to remember here on Earth—*1) spiritually, 2) mentally, 3) physically.*

1) *To remember by spirit is to simply know, to know by Grace.* If we are born knowing something, that means we earned it in a past life, we own it on a soul level. We were therefore allowed to bring it up on line in this life, gratis. For example, when I was a little boy, my mother told me it was impolite to point at someone. I didn't point at anyone until I was 32 years old. It's an awesome power to point at someone.

To point at someone, by the way, is a form of intimi-dation/energy-theft, words having failed to impose one's will over another. It is now time for the electromagnetic manipulation of the etheric energy field. Conducting this energy out of the index finger is the first veiled threat of violence.

How I learned the pointing lesson: I had a high fever, then hypothermia. My body had gone into spasm (and not the kind of spasm we like).

One of the spasms landed me in a past life in 1813. I was a settler in a little town; I found myself admonishing this gun slinger for spitting on the wooden sidewalk. I drew my index finger and shook it at him repeatedly. Rather than engage me in conversation, he merely drew his weapon and shot me. My coat flew open as I fell backward. Blood saturated the shirt in moments. Then the gentlest little autumn breeze sent me into hypothermia. I spasmed and died; talk about cold blood!

So when Mom told me not to point, I had that one up in a nanosecond.

2) *Remembering with the brain.* If you do not know the lesson in spirit, it becomes your *brain's turn to remember.* Whatever input your brain has (books, TV, friends, spirit guides, music, etc.) becomes saturated with remembering. Your spirit guides will spare no opportunity to put reminders in your path. In failing to remember the lesson with your mind, which, by the way, was a very popular thing to do down here (let's face it, it was a vogue), you demote the process one more level and it then becomes your body's turn to remember the lesson. Please write on a piece of paper hundreds of times, "It is safe for me to no longer be tangled in my own mind."

3) *Remembering with your body* can be quite uncomfortable. I'm not going to discount that you can remember from joy; however the body's main method of helping you remember is to put you in pain. Ever notice how people in agony seem to have more open minds? What do I have to do to stop this pain? Change my belief system? Remember a lesson! "I'll think about it . . ." This answer may not serve you very well; simply choose to remember.

Different parts of the body help you learn different lessons. The job of the pancreas is to illustrate self-indulgence teachings. Now, if you have spent a lifetime failing at this lesson, failing to control self-indulgence, the pancreas may create diabetes. Oh, you don't want to look at that; well, blindness is a symptom of diabetes. Yes, you'll be looking at that. Yes, you will have to control sugar self-indulgence if you wish to continue to live. When the body has been assigned the task of remembering, reality may look like change, or pain, or even threat of death.

Anything to do with the lungs is a "love of life" lesson. That is the breath of life. If you have ever heard someone awakening, he or she draws in a sharp breath. This is the body welcoming the soul back from its astral journey. Look at the gesture of flicking an ash off the end of a cigarette as contempt for life itself. The soul that creates pneumonia is the soul who has forgotten to love our fellow humans. Pneumonia is a disease of resentment.

Any chronic pain is the result of refusing to remember a lesson again and again. Lower back pain is created by bending over backward to please someone. It's the happiness lesson. You can't make someone else happy. Other people either are or are not happy! Your happiness is a decision you are responsible to make for yourself, someone else can't do it. Get over "trying" to make someone happy.

Not remembering that *happiness is internal, not external*, may result in a lifetime of chronic back pain. Actually snap the spine, what's it gonna take? The body only ups the ante again and again, until either we remember or decide on that option about beginning all over again as a child; perhaps a child with childhood diabetes.

Personally, I'm happy to hear about childhood diabetes. It means some soul said, "frontload the self-indulgence remembering for me would ya?" A childhood with no candy, that could serve to remind one of the self-indulgence lesson right away. It's good to see someone "get on the stick!"

Let's talk about Alzheimer's: in this case, the souls in question have spent a lifetime refusing to change the programming, period. They have provided so much resistance that the job of evolution is turned over to the body in total. The first play that the body makes is to snip off the brain, delete all the files. After all, it has been the brain that was in the way the entire time. Then the body dies of whatever the most indicative malady might be.

As a final example, the common cold. The common cold is a vacation from life that we force the body to take. The body has taken over for the brain. We all require occasional "down time." In other words, the cold is three days where you are very kind to yourself. There you are, nestled in your own personal ashram, doing that very cleansing, single nostril breathing technique (preferred by yogis 10 out of 10 times).

What actually happened is that the body created the time off. Rather than creating time off with your mind by calling your boss and saying, "I feel very, very well today and I feel like I could use some time for me, see you Thursday," the vacation created by the body, not the mind, is spent on the bench, not the beach.

All malfunctions of the body equal some form of amnesia. You have forgotten to love some part of yourself.

Readers are welcome to contact me and ask about the spiritual cause of any disease: write me in care of the publisher. All sickness is from the past—a unhealed trauma.

Okay, for the hard-bitten scientist out there—why did you, at that time, create an environment in your body that fostered the growth of that particular germ? That is, as opposed to the other millions of germs we are exposed to daily. Why not the week before, or a week hence? The answer is "not acknowledging the desire for time for yourself" created the environment.

As for germs, they have no idea they're germs; they are just somebody looking for lunch. We, in our judgment of them, create them as evil, and in doing so give them more credit than they deserve. What we judge sticks to us. Judging germs sticks them to us. After all, they really only serve to build up our immune system anyway. *All microbes are our little buddies.*

I gotta hand it to the gypsies; they really see us coming. They tell us that nothing that's wrong in our life is our fault; it's not our doing. Our life is not our responsibility. Everything that is wrong has happened because someone else put an evil spell on us. "$49.95 and they'll burn a candle."

This paragraph is sarcasm. *We buy it every time, after all, how could anything wrong in our life be our fault? Somebody else must be doing it! (It's the germs' fault we're sick. Ya, that's it. We're just a victim of circumstances. How could our being sick have been created by anything but germs. Certainly we didn't do it!) Then we "magically" make everything in our life all right again. Still asleep, we then credit the gypsy's candle or the doctor's pill. There's no difference.*

So the next time you get sick, give yourself a little credit. You created this illness, not the germ. You did it by not remembering something. It's your creation, be proud of it. And not just when you boast about it, as you call in sick.

Realize that getting sick is a decision and only a decision. Go back and pinpoint the exact moment you made the decision to become sick. Now make a different decision, choose to remember without having to involve the body in the process. It's only a decision; *it's that simple; just make it.*

Body-of-Evidence Thinking

To begin this section, let's define the word "skeptic." This term is indicative of a person who has a huge hyperactive left brain, and a little iddy-biddy dysfunctional right brain. So the next time we hear people identify themselves as skeptical, thank them for admitting they think with half a brain. Doubt is a barrier to progress.

Well, we were pretty much all going through life with our thinking based on our experience, "the body of evidence." So let me ask you all to think of a time when life was unfair. Now let me ask if life is unfair. If we say, "Yes," guess what we create?

This is called "circular logic." The body of evidence only creates more evidence, not progress. How do we fix it? The word would be "arbitrarily!" "I arbitrarily choose and create a life in which I am supported by people who are awake, magnificent, watching miracles occurring 24 hours a day! I choose, intend, and invest in boldly creating a much higher consciousness in myself. I do this effortlessly, by Grace. Thank you, angels, thank me, myself. This is my reality, even though the body of evidence states otherwise." By the way, whenever you hear the phrase "even though," it is evidence that the user is trapped in circular logic.

Now if you say something like, "everyone in this room is asleep except myself," then you have created a "locked-in-stone" concept. No matter how much everyone else wakes up, they can only be asleep in your reality. However, if you say they "seem or appear" to be asleep, then your remark is in a liquid form and can change. "Seem" and "appear" act like etheric lubricants.

Hope
Why would hope be listed as a word of disempowerment? If you have faith, knowing that everything is perfect, then hope is a real non-issue. Therefore hope can be seen as an affirmation of doubt. Well, at least I hope so.

Section III

Positive Patterning

WORDS OF EMPOWERMENT

NOW LET US INTRODUCE some very powerful images and words. Let's start in the computer part of the brain. Pop in the disk titled "How I Make Money." If we open the program, it may say something like, "You make money working for someone else doing something you have no real feeling for." If we peel back the program another layer, we may find a Puritan standing there, telling us that we must suffer in order to get money, and then not even enough money to make ends meet. Job = Just over broke.

Effortlessness

Let's just dump that program in the trash. I will discuss money ideas and images that will empower us—that will bring pleasant changes into our lives from here on out. Our new four-word program, "I make money *effortlessly*," will change us completely. The way that the old program functioned meant that money could come only through a narrow slot. The new program allows money to come from all directions. If one does what one loves in life, it is inherently effortless. When one, through personal will ("willful behavior") attempts to make something happen, when the timing isn't synchronized, great resistance occurs.

Timing is everything. If it isn't the right time, you may apply as much will as you want and it still won't happen. Replace "willfulness" with the concept "allow." The use of the word "effortlessness" will delete willfulness, as in, "I move through traffic effortlessly." After all, tension is just misplaced attention.

Rebirthing!

Rebirthing = unconscious reprogramming. We are warm, safe, and surrounded by love. We are in the womb. Then suddenly one day it's show time. We are yanked into subzero weather, a bright light put in our brand new eyes. Someone 40 times our size holds us upside down, assaulting us. Someone else is cutting off our connection to the universe, the umbilical cord. All the while we are choking on the amniotic fluid in our lungs. This is the first touch of our fellow beings, the first programming we receive in life (and obviosly your author is not bitter about it at all). The program looks like the world is not a safe place and everybody is out to get us. We all act out this programming unconsciously until we die or reprogram. This is why no one can feel safe if life gets good. We unconsciously anticipate the upcoming birth trauma.

The character of Al Bundy on the program "Married with Children" got a lucky streak. He drew a royal flush in a high-stakes poker game. When he drew the last card, what came out of his mouth? Was it, "God I'm lucky. What a miracle!?" No, he said, "I'm doomed." Something that fortunate would have to equal a trauma that would kill him. On the show, the game was raided as per his unconscious request.

Life never again appears to be as good as it was in the womb. Therefore, when things begin to go very well, we won't even talk about it. We are afraid of calling the doom.

Can we see this in our lives? We who do rebirthing don't wish to hang anyone out to dry. The solution is to reprogram our unconscious mind. This is done very efficiently by writing affirmations on paper. We write them many, many times, just as we did as children in school.

Dearest reader, if you get a notebook for just this purpose and write, "*I am pleasing to myself and others,*" this will begin the reprogramming.

The rebirthing is a breath technique that enables us to actually see moments in life where trauma caused us to write "internal paradigm." Then an individual affirmation is coined to do away with the subsequent negative behavior.

For example, if the doctor that delivered us said something like, "the baby will be all right on its own now," while taking us away from Mom, for the rest of our life the internal paradigm states that we have to do everything ourselves. We can never receive help. All the weight is on our shoulders.

The correcting programming may sound like, "It is safe for me to receive assistance from others," if this sounds like you. In other words, you have to do everything around the house or at work yourself. No one even thanks or acknowledges you. Then boldly experiment. Write the affirmation 1,000 times, and see if there is a change.

Personally, I love to use children's composition books. They are inexpensive. At this writing, I may have filled twenty of them, cover to cover, with my personal reprograms. I have successfully abolished internal paradigm after internal paradigm. I can actually write, "Every day is my fortunate day!" This was after fourteen months of rebirthing. I now get up to see what my good fortune will be today.

If rebirthing has struck a chord, please contact me or any rebirther. As soon as contact is made, the process begins.

I am happy with myself,
I am satisfied with my life.

Self-Love = Self-Discipline; Discipline = Intent

Those of us who are raising children realize that the children we love wish to have borders set for them. They are not yet old enough to set the boundries for themselves. Because we love them, we are prepared to set and enforce these borders for them.

Let's do this for ourselves as adults. The children are not old enough to recognize, for example, the danger of cars in the street. So we explain not to run out without looking. We are prepared to physically stop them. In applying this love principal to ourselves, it is obvious that we can set borders for ourselves.

Since we are adults, we can choose to enforce them for ourselves. This is called personal sovereignty. Therefore, self-love equals self-discipline. The discipline is the intent we have for our self-realization. Discipline is enforcing our own borders through love (for self).

Love of Self and Love of Others is Synonymous

I have a friend who journeyed to Mexico. He laid down big bucks to have a private session with Max, the Maya Crystal Skull. During this time he had a quartz crystal sphere in his pocket.

He puts the sphere in my hands. I am instantly looking into the eyes of the crystal skull. I go to the "place where children play." It is set up like a temple. We kids are in the central hall. I'm not the oldest kid, I'm not the youngest kid. I had at first thought there was sunlight streaming between the pillars. It turned out that the pillars were light beings and the spaces between them were not as bright. We play! I come back apparently about a half hour later. The border between self-love and love of others has totally vanished. If you love self, there is benefit; if you love others, there is benefit. It's all the same.

NO

It is safe to say NO! In owning your own power, it serves you best to no longer become involved in others' fear. Especially their fear of manifestation. The old paradigm was, "If I say no, I'm a bad person." "I am guilty." Untrue. You are a very good person. Saying no is sometimes quite appropriate.

Were you to say no, and the other chooses anger as his or her reaction, the real question is, "What fear is in his or her driver's seat?"

Other peoples' opinion of you is much more likely to be an opinion of themselves than of you. Other peoples' opinion of you isn't even your business. Let me phrase it another way: who's opinion of any one of us is the only opinion that counts? Saying no serves to detangle us effortlessly. *You may choose to do only that which you love.*

YES

Giving and receiving is the quintessential breath of the universe. When we receive, the world is a better place. When someone offers us an energy-theft and we say yes, this may not serve us very well. The age of energy-theft is long gone.

I have offered gifts and had them refused. This is perfect. I choose many moments to take the opportunity to be generous. Generosity is an attribute of strength, not weakness. Discernment plays the pivotal role. There are times to be generous; there are times not to be generous.

It Is Safe to No Longer Be Tangled in Our Own Minds!

(Who's mind is it anyway?) Our minds can be beautiful places. We realize that the old thinking no longer works, and choose to change it. If we examine the old thinking, it may turn out that it isn't our thinking. It's someone else's thinking. That thinking did not work for the people that gave it to us and doesn't work for us either. Any thought that makes us feel bad is a fear, a tangle. Remember to recognize and dismiss fear thoughts.

You can choose to think or not to think anything. If you say, "I can't help what I think," then who is doing the thinking? It's time to choose to think for yourself. Technically, fear used to be doing almost all the thinking for you. How boring! Invent "Braino," that's cream rinse for the mind. Here is a dose—please say this out loud—"I change my way of thinking by Grace, effortlessly, thank you."

The Four Methods of Energy Theft
Many Thanks and Great Honors to James Redfield

1) *Ah—Poor Me:* This is where we whine some excuse about why we don't have enough. This may be better known as complaining. The person we whine to is expected to give in to, and underwrite, the whiner. As we realize that everyone has 100 percent of what we require already, internally, energy-theft disappears.

2) *The Elitist:* This situation takes place when someone doesn't respond to us and we have to expend even more

energy. For example, someone doesn't return our call. Then we have to call again. This is the comparison game.

3) *The Interrogator:* Someone makes us wrong by asking questions that he or she has no business asking. It steals our energy. Almost any personal question is in this category, especially with those we love.

Why haven't you finished this book yet? An answer that may serve us best would be, "Frankly it's none of your business. Had it been your business, I would have volunteered the information."

4) *The Intimidator:* "Give me your lunch money or I will beat you up." It has been exactly the same since grade school. Bullies search for passive victims. I believe it is the Mahatma who modeled the correct approach: "I will not cooperate with you, go ahead and kill me." The enzyme that makes this work is faith. Were we to choose this passive resistance, the situation itself would be forced to transmute. We are habituated to give away our power. It is the unhealed unconscious that calls the bully to begin with. We are in a free-will zone. Own it and we are bully proof.

It is the opinion of your author that a fifth form of energy-theft exists which looks like any form of expectation. If you expect something from another, you create a harmonic between the two that serves neither.

As long as your subconscious remains programmed to respond to these energy thefts, you will continue to create victimhood. The section on rebirthing addresses reprogramming the subconscious.

Top Eleven Reasons You Know
You've Been a UFO Abductee

11) All the other members of your abductee support group think you're the one who's nuts.

10) Whenever anyone takes your picture with a flash, you can't remember the next three hours.

9) Your car now gets lightyears to the gallon.

8) When someone yells, "Look—A flying saucer!" and you hear yourself say, "Ya, been there, done that."

7) You never replace light bulbs anymore, because you can read by your aura.

6) You rub your forehead after a gust of wind because you got something in your Third Eye.

5) You feel as if you've had a medical exam, but you can't find the bill.

4) Every time you go up in an elevator, you ask to get off on the floor with the little green men.

3) Your implants require watering.

2) Whenever anyone asks what time it is, you go into a deep philosophical meditation.

The number 1 reason you know you've been abducted by aliens:

1) It's the best excuse you could think of to give your spouse at the time, but then you begin to wonder . . .

Crystal Grid

There are many books written about crystals. One thing that you do with crystals is spread them out around the house in a specific way. To form a crystal grid is to place the stones in a specific sacred geometric form, focused with a specific intent. There are countless applications. They cast into 3-D a harmonious energy field designed to work in a specific way. That "way" is by your design.

You can, for example, place four crystals at the four corners of your property. Each point of the crystal is aimed at 45 degrees, making an X over the whole property. The house (your sacred space) is then sealed with your intent.

You begin by holding the crystals in your hands and telling the crystals what kind of a grid they are going to cast. Tell them to create a space in which the frequency is held higher, so that all who come here are healed. The perimeters of time can be altered. You create your reality in each moment. When you change your reality, all reality is changed. Your reality is your beliefs. Change them and all the world changes, since you cocreate reality as a group. The only reality you can change is your own.

If you are choosing to grid the four corners of the property, it may be done by ceremony. This may look like gathering friends of like mind together. Call the elementals to assist. Fire, earth, air, and water may be called by the law of similarities.

First dig a hole a few inches deep, place the crystal at the 45-degree angle and bury the crystal. (If you move, it would be ethical to remove the grid.) Then light a small candle, placed directly above the crystal. Then draw a circle around the candle with sea salt. Then circle it again with water. Then, to call the element of air, place a stick of incense in the circle. Say a blessing for the house out loud.

Programming I have placed in my crystal grid: the highest light, safety, joy, completion, superior choice, money, Maya Time, all who come here shall heal. Add to this whatever specific requests you desire to make to the universe.

Alternate Incarnations

Many people have asked whether or not we have past lives. Did I have past life? Let me tell you that you did! The church, in its control games, are causing people to question whether or not they had past lives.

The more appropriate question is: *Who was I in my past lives?* There are similarities between who one is now and who one was in those other lives. These similarities and differences relate to the evolution of the soul.

The true essence of life, true evolution, is the remembering process. You choose certain lessons to remember in each given lifetime. As many lifetimes as are required are created in order to remember them. Your current life is the lifetime in which you remember it all.

Perhaps patterns that repeat themselves in your present life have become visible. *These negative patterns represent unconscious mind programming.* Looking at a life where the programming is different is astoundingly helpful.

Multidimensional life-viewing provides us with the objective witness viewpoint. The great grace of alternate life exploration is that the chosen reactions to the patterns (programming) and the ramifications of the choices become apparent as the whole of the lifetime is viewed.

Other incarnations reveal a series of events that help reveal where the patterns in the current life come from. A future life may hold a particular remembering. We can return from the future to the present with this memory up on line. In other words, if we are healed in a future life, we can go and get that healing. We can make a different choice, have a different reaction, and actually remember the lesson rhymed in the pattern.

Let's use the "broken heart" as an example. Let's say that in a past incarnation you fall in love with someone else. This person leaves to go to war. Broken-hearted, you "wait." Eventually your life becomes "waiting," and nothing else. You get very comfortable in this self-imposed state.

You think that when the other person gets back, then you will be whole, complete. The reality of your life, however, is sitting on the front porch watching the road that your lover may someday walk down. Meanwhile, forty years go by. Now you return to the current life to find that, indeed, the same person is again a player. Your love for this person is again a reality, and again he or she has gone away.

Well, we gotta ask: How many years does one warm the bench in this lifetime? Answer: Zero!

The broken heart is healed at the moment that it is no longer waiting for the other person to be complete, to function. We can all find our own teachers. We can all support ourselves. We are all whole within ourselves now in this moment.

There is no doubt that human beings are designed to pair up. However, any one of us is complete within our own life, and we each have everything required to be whole. Love has been perverted into codependency in this society. The time for the healing has arrived. We have re-membered to be complete within ourselves. Now two whole people can join forces toward a greater goal. Spin-ning our wheels in the codependency pattern creates energy-theft. Classically, one provides energy so the other person can become "whole." That never happens; more and more energy is given, with no return. Eventually, one partner becomes exhausted and creates leaving or dying.

All of our lives are occurring simultaneously. It's easy to explore on either side of the "now." I have accompa-nied thousands of people into their future incarnations. Major trends have been observed. The vast majority who land in bodies on Earth, land in an "Atlantian-like" cul-ture. They describe healing pyramids, and a society based on peace not war. Connection with alien civilizations is a given. Reality is based on consensus. I'm happy to report that we are moving toward a very bright and fulfilling future.

The soul, over the timeline, has projected many bodies. It is no trick at all to project two at the same time, and in two different locations. Your soul may be projecting a body in some other country, or as another gender, or on another planet, as we speak. In fact, there is a vertical axis, as well, that allows experiencing the self in other dimen-sions. The concept of past lives is now called multidimen-sional consciousness, and we are all capable of exploring it. How do you begin the journey? Ask the question, "Who was I in my past lives?"

Safety/Trust

You are safe or you are not safe. It has nothing to do with where you are or who you are with. It is another one of these internal concepts. Everywhere is your Universe. You decide if you are safe in your universe or not. I am safe in my Universe. You may have walked through downtown Saigon during a bombing raid, without Scratch One, and yet have been mugged in a suburban shopping mall. Just decide that you are safe.

Trust is in the same internal category. You can trust all other people by assuming that they are in the perfect place on their evolutionary curve. The question is, do you want to play with them where they're at?

All lessons are remembered as though in a 360-degree circle. If someone is at, say, 70 degrees in the personal hygiene lesson (they stink) and you are, say, up around 350, then you would have to ratchet down to work with the person. This may not be appropriate. Someone around 100 degrees would serve better to work with that person. You, through your discernment, may choose not to play with this person, without making the person wrong. Trust looks like observing where others appear to be on their individual learning curve. Trust is trust in your own discernment. Do trust your own discernment.

Power

Everyone is talking about owning one's power. How I remembered the word "own." I was in drive time. I had a fear that affected every cell, every atom in my body. I had to pull over; however, I owned that fear, totally. There was no uncertainty, there was no doubt. This is what I mean by "own."

Power equals your gifts, talents, and abilities. These are easy to own. What is even easier to own is true human power. It is akin to God. It is the ability to generate and beam love. You can generate love that never existed before. When you do this, you are God, you are creating the Universe.

Once upon a time, there was a man who was helping his girlfriend move to a new home. As he was loading boxes onto the truck, her former husband came across the front lawn and pointed a gun at the man. The man said, "I love you." At this, the former husband turned white and stumbled away. He asked the girlfriend what had just happened.

She said that she was there and she had been looking in the mind of her former husband, and when the man said, "I love you," he vanished, became invisible in front of the former husband. "I love you" would not compute in his brain, so he could not see the man who said it. When the man decided to make love not war, he literally disappeared. The former husband saw the truck right through the man. The former husband didn't even remember the incident.

Choice is an astounding power when we remember to choose the most loving response no matter what the stimulation is. We are omnipotent. *Our true power is our ability to generate and beam love! Own it.*

Imagination: The Only Place in the Human Mind Where There are No Limits

Very interesting word—imagination. It is your connection to "source." It is the ability to focus. Imagination is the most powerful thing in the Universe. It is even more powerful than God. One could imagine that God does not exist, and create that as a reality. Imagine that. It is one's true power, it is *magic*.

One could imagine oneself well, or rich, or happy. In fact, to be all those things, to create such a reality, one must imagine. By the use of the imagination, in a nanosecond one could be standing on the planet Uranus and come back. It takes light-minutes to go from the Sun to that planet.

Therefore, the forces that (used to) be have tried to disempower the word, as in, "It's only your imagination." Ya, right.

Imagination had been tied up with the "what-if" syndrome. You have been asked to use the imagination to create a dark future. How often does this worst-case scenario actually happen anyway?

Here is another scenario: when we are children, still creating in our divinity, we speak words to create the future. In "futuring," children talk about things that don't exist yet. Parents admonish us greatly for lying. We are raised with creativity = lying. Not anymore we aren't.

Choice
We have been programmed for our entire lifetime, both socially and genetically, to have certain reactions. We are used to mindlessly acting out the unconscious programming *du jour*. We no longer have to do this. We no longer do this. That is what choice means. This programming isn't our own. It isn't our thinking. It is stuff we have been told since childhood.

Our brain tells us that we can't wake up without a cup of coffee. Pardon me, are we awake when we have that thought? What are the coffee cartels doing in my kitchen? The next time the brain impulses a choice (decision) like that, ask who is speaking. Is that you, Juan Valdez? Give yourself permission to make a different choice. It's okay. We no longer choose to be programmed with this old thinking that doesn't work anyway (say rebirthing).

Meditation
The word "meditation" means to listen. It is a method by which we connect to source. Meditating on a regular basis is a key to greater ascension. Find a comfortable place to regularly meditate. It may be essential to start the meditation with the sentence "I, for the next little while, will not be concerned with the cares of the world. This is time for me. Some being of the highest light speaks to me. I intend to hear you. Thanks." Spirit guides and angels are always standing by to assist in our evolution. In many ways, they are our greatest allies.

The Parable of the Barbarian
For many years, I performed the Opening of the Third Eye Ceremony. In this event, the person envisions a beautiful

field in which there are birds, butterflies, wild flowers, a warm afternoon sun, and a complete feeling of safety. Suddenly, in meditation, I find myself in this field. Christ, Himself, walks with me. I tell Him that I am troubled by having done so many events over the years where less people show up than had agreed to come. He says "Come with me."

Next I see a barbarian, poised ready to knock down a door and sack a city. In looking inside the barbarian, one observes a less than superior brain. In fact, the adjective stupid would not be inappropriate. Yet within his matrix is such a fixed purpose of mind that he would have to literally be killed in order to keep him from knocking down that door.

We, in this modern time, experience gaining higher consciousness by sticking one toe in. Then we wait six months. Then two toes, then another six months. Our barbarian seems to have an ability that we don't have. What if we chose working on ourselves with that same fixed purpose of mind that the barbarian so easily held? So much so that nothing would stop us from holding higher frequency!

Rebirthing is the re-righting of the dysfunctional unconscious mind. When I begin my own rebirthing, I put up so much resistance that I became carsick on the way to the event. Rebirthing is certainly one of the greatest things I do for myself and therefore I came up with the perfect excuse not to do it (car sickness). In fact, the more excuses that one may find not to do something, the greater the good it will do. It is in inverse mathematical ratio. These excuses are in reality fear *per sé. I boldly embrace becoming conscious. I change effortlessly by Grace!*

Faith

For many years, I prayed to be able to teach the subject of Faith. Finally my prayers are answered! Can you recall a moment in life where you just knew that everything would work out perfectly, that you weren't really in trouble? Everyone around you was convinced that you were in deep feces, yet somehow you knew better. Now imagine that concept as 24-7. You spend all of your time knowing that everything has worked out perfectly. This is called faith. You can live it, and in fact, it is effortless! (Observe the number of excuses found not to have faith.) I reiterate: Twenty-four hours a day, seven days a week, you have perfect knowing that everything is working out perfectly right now. This state of mind is referred to as faith.

Responsibility

Responsibility is the ability to respond. We all have such an ability in abundance. This word may have been used to rob us of our power, especially around the time you decided to desire a pet. Whenever it is used, there is an implied lack of this ability. What fiction we write.

Intimacy

Intimacy means "into-me-see." It is long past the age of secrecy. There are no secrets in the universe. Good, now we can all see into each other. It is more difficult not to see into our fellow being. *The party has begun!*

Intelligence

I have been musing with the Mensa Books. They have about a hundred different philosophers and scholars who have been quoted with their different definitions of intelligence. Therefore I came up with my own. I mean seize an opportunity. Intelligence is the ability to recognize and seize opportunity, period. In other words, grab that carp! And, by the way, thanks for reading this book.

Section IV

Creativity
and Satisfaction

WORDS OF THE NEW PARADIGM

HERETOFORE, WE HAVE BEEN deleting dysfunctional words and adding ones that serve us in a much better fashion. This section is a departure. Here we are actually suggesting new vistas of thought—new constructs of limitations we have had our entire lives. We are talking about actual freedom!

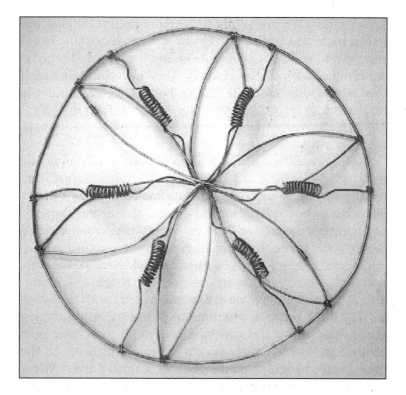

Plans

Those of us involved in raising children will easily realize that any plans we make will undoubtedly go askew. It is only after we have blessed all possible outcomes that we can choose. If we insist that reality will go in one and only one way, we evoke the law of resistance. "Whatever we resist will persist."

It is by loving all possible outcomes, by blessing all possible contingencies, that we are free to choose. This may be explained by the phrase "detaching from outcome." Being attached to only a certain outcome is *lack mentality*, as such. *Bless it all, and then choose.*

Boy, Girl, Other

As we know, we are all divine souls, a perfect balance between male and female energy. In order to incarnate, however, we have to make a call on the gender of the body. Around the turn of this century, they began to issue each soul two bodies. Into the female body, they (we) put the male energy. Into the male body goes the female energy. All men are really women, and all women are really men, energetically.

This means that if you are male, your female built the male body. She built it according to her view of men. Personally, my male persona is handsome enough. She didn't allow me to be too handsome. I am tall and slender, however, I had been ineffective. That is the way my female views a "safe" male. When I was in high school, I watched all my buddies build absolutely gorgeous "muscleman" bodies. Me, nothing—I lifted the same number of weights, nothing. This is because my female associates muscles with brutality.

The body we're in attempts to please the soul occupying it. This is, by the way, the reason all men have gorgeous legs. Many female bodies grow a mustache. In the male camp, weight, volume of flesh, equals power. Many male souls were embarrassed to be in one of those little female bodies, so the body was bulked up. In that way, there would be weight to throw around. In the female camp, slender equals power.

This had been perhaps the very first step in the evolution of the human species becoming androgynous. The vast majority of species in the universe are androgynous. This is clearly the more evolved form. Fifty years ago, a baby born with both sets of genitalia was one in a million. These days it is one in a thousand. They always make the baby female because the surgery is easier. Three hundred years hence the majority of people on Earth will be in androgynous bodies. If we've seen racism, sexism, homophobia, et al, imagine androgenaphobia, not.

In our lifetime, we have seen the total dissolution of gender roles. You can be male and do any job, you can be female and do any job. That was so long ago.

Have you noticed the new kids on the block? The teenagers? America is the only country in the world that uses the word teenager. It is a word of disempowerment, bigtime. If you can tell what gender a young adult is, it annoys them. Then they go get another piercing. The guys are wearing skirts called kilts. Male-polish is surging in the market. All females are cross-dressers. Outfits that would make a lumberjack proud are a standard mode of dress for women.

Those of us already owning our androgyny seem to pair with someone who is polarized male or polarized female. It is for us to demonstrate to them that it is safe to function in either modality, depending on the situation. It may seem boring to us because the polarity of the other forces us to play only one role. Were two androgynes to pair, we would be less effective in the formula.

A true healing of this is to know that women are born with 100 percent of the male attributes up on line and functioning. And vice versa. In seminars, I ask females if they would allow a man to totally support them financially. I get a NO that would knock you off the podium. Financial support has been a traditional male energy. When I ask the males if they would allow a woman to totally support them I get answers like: "Who is this woman?" "Do you have a phone number?"

Remember that in order to put up the other gender's attributes it is not necessary to take anything off line. The other gender's matrix is added to what one already has. There is no pendulum swing. There is only balance.

Sex, Sex, Sex

You began reading right here didn't you? We are such fun-seekers. Pardon the energy-theft by interrogation. It was too funny. I just didn't resist.

Sex was invented in order that the body itself may share in the love we feel for another soul. When we "make love," we do exactly that. We make love! Love is generated in the process. One becomes elated by this love. When we make love, a spiral of energy going up is created in the astral plane. If there is conception, a soul rides that spiral down into incarnation.

The reason sex is so forbidden is that it is just that important. It is holy. It is sacred. In making love, dimensional doors open. Making love is a divine meditation. It connects us to our own higher frequencies.

In the third century, a college of cardinals announced that if a woman were to have an orgasm with a man, then that man could steal her soul. Of course, the Church-Establishment-Herd "tried" to make sex wrong. Of course they failed. Our being forbidden to do it guaranteed our participation. In fact, technically, the word forbidden means "do it covertly."

The Victorians took suppression to a new height. At one time, the entire Earth was enveloped in the thought form of sexual taboo. Sex is in no way dirty, wrong, nor will you go blind.

Sexual repression is no longer the norm. Do we not adore the sensual among us? All, ALL, A-L-L sexual taboo is a myth when love is involved. Remember to enjoy love. Love your body. Love for your body! Your body loves you, too.

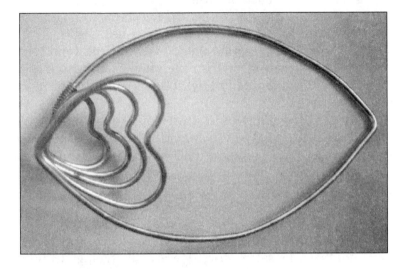

Telepathic Powers

The human species is far more telepathically linked than you know. People simply have no words to own it. It has been kept virtually invisible. Let's say that you are very in love with someone. That means that you are *very* telepathically linked with that person.

Now let's say that your loved one is delayed in arriving. Naturally, you check in with this person telepathically, and you "hear" your loved one say something like, "Sorry, Darling, I'll be there in an hour."

You actually *heard* your loved one say that he or she is delayed, yet you continue to pace.

If the telephone had rung, and you had physically heard your loved one say this, then the pacing would stop. However, you have already "heard" the message! *You don't trust*, or own, your own telepathic ability. Yet it works perfectly! And it is free.

We all have friends. We'll be thinking about someone and then the phone rings. It's your friend! We were actually in telepathic broadcast until the phone rang.

We have been ripped off by the telephone company for our telepathic ability. (Does this ring a bell?) How about owning our own telepathic ability? We may trust our telepathic ability even more than the phone company. There are virtually no words in English describing this form of communication.

Telepathic dialing—as it turns out, that old witchy saying was true. Say my name out loud three times, feel the love between us, and I will come lovingly to speak with you. This is called 1-800-IAMU. We are all perfectly telepathically linked.

Satisfaction Breath

No amount of food, money, sex, drugs, alcohol, cigarettes, etc., will ever be satisfactory. We are all "trying" to fill a void that does not exist. Once more, we have been tricked. *It suddenly becomes obvious that satisfaction is internal, not external. We are satisfied or we are not.*

Back in the 30s, Lucky Strike cigarettes came out with the "Smoking Satisfaction" advertising campaign. They really blew us a lot of smoke all right. What we're calling satisfaction breath is similar to a drag on a cigarette, only without the smoke.

Sometimes in the process of falling asleep, we inhale deeply and release it with a feeling of Ahhhh. This is a satisfaction breath. If you choose, do one now. Inhale through the nose until the lungs are completely filled. The ribs feel a sensation of joy. Release through the nose, with an ahhh . . . It feels truly wonderful. It is internal satisfaction. Enjoy it; do it often. It is true satisfaction. It is all we really require to be able to own "I am satisfied with my life." It creates balance in a life that may have had the odds stacked against it.

You can disconnect from any feeling of lack by thinking of it and taking a satisfaction breath. It is renewal itself.

Enjoy true breathing satisfaction
Anytime and it's free as well as freeing.

Our breath may be used to ground intent. Think of an intent. Now simply breathe it into existence . . . It is that easy.

Breathairian: Take seven satisfaction breaths in a row, hold the last inhalalation and program the body to be "nourished." Then as you exhale you are full, fulfilled, fully.

Time

When we are small children, we exist in a blissful state of timelessness. When we learn to read a clock, then we are on the clock for the rest of our lives. When Mommy or Daddy says it is time to go to bed, we have no idea of what they are talking about. After all, we've just spent all day getting in this good mood. And so, the resentment of time begins. As an adult, we may have become chronically late, or chronically early. This is also a resentment of time, the unconscious rebellion.

First of all, we have never been given any information about time. When the hand of a clock moves an eighth of an inch, we say a minute has gone by. This isn't true. What has happened is that the machine called a clock has measured an eighth of an inch of space, not time.

Naturally, the question arises, "What is time?" Time is art. Did you feel that in your body? Then time is used to create, masterfully. It is certain that time is not money. That is one of the biggest ripoffs there is. Time is consciousness. We create consciousness.

Time, in the sense of the universe, is pulsation emitted consistently at a fixed rate. A quartz-crystal watch is an example. Time travels through the galaxy in wave form. The idea is to "catch the wave," and ride it. Time really has nothing to do with space. Travel in space is hopping from one place to another effortlessly by thought, within the same wave.

The education we have been given did not actually differentiate time and space; when our vehicle slows in traffic (slows down in space) we may have reacted by actually slowing down time. Anger always equals uninformed. And so the lack of education about time is the true source of the enormous frustration we all feel in a traffic jam.

Time Traveling

Since you create consciousness, you also create time. For example, if you have ever had a job where you go home at exactly 5 o'clock, one minute to 5 was the longest minute in that day. How is this possible? How can it vary like that? It is the consciousness that varies.

If you are in the now, being where you want to be, and doing what you love to do, you are in a state of timelessness. Just like the pre-time child.

Have you had the experience of taking a familiar journey and found that somehow the trip took significantly less time than normal? What happened? You didn't necessarily speed. Again it was the consciousness. Observe how you expand and contract time. If you are having a good time, it flies by. If you are going somewhere you don't want to go, time, and the journey drags and drags.

If you see a road sign that says 212 miles to Manhattan, you program in so many spins of the tires, so much gas, so many hours. Because you unconsciously program this stuff, that becomes the reality. You even program in the exact moment your butt becomes sore. You are trapped in linear time. The trap is the "waiting" to arrive. When you are in the "now" then you are in a constant state of "arrived."

How does one program in a different reality? How can I do this by will? OOPS, meant to say "free will." How do you choose to arrive at your local destination on time? This article isn't really an excerpt from "Jeopardy." However the answer is: What is fixed design? Fixed design is Sacred Geometry, the underpinning of the universe, combined with desire and intent.

How do I time travel in my vehicle in reality? Build the time bubble around the car. Inside the car, time passes at a different rate than time outside the car. It is not about the clock. It isn't about the speedometer/odometer, it is about the flow. It is about play, enjoyment. Good music will help. You will arrive timelessly. The trick is to remain in the now. As soon as you pause to look at the speedometer or clock, or even think about what percentage of the journey remains, you no longer exit in the now, the timelessness. The wavespell has been broken.

Once you have taught a child how to tell time and then take the child somewhere in the car, all you hear is, "Are we there yet? Are we there yet?" The child was successfully trapped in time and is reflecting your frustration back to you. Life is, after all, the celebration of the journey, not the measurement to the destination.

We are modeling a new understanding of time. That is fourth-dimensional time. This is the application of Love Consciousness in every situation. Let's just call it galactic time, or time-consciousness.

As the galaxy may have been created by the sudden expansion of matter (the Big Bang Theory), the universe then modeled time for us. Think of time as an ever-expanding sphere, with the very epicenter of the sphere being the moment now. And the surface of the sphere is the future. The idea of travel through space becomes choosing the most convenient radii to get to the point on the surface that you have chosen. This time sphere is the model for the time bubble around the three-dimensional car.

In linear time, the only way to get from portal A to portal B is to travel in a straight line. We appeared to have been trapped on the timeline, as though along a single diameter in the sphere, as on the face of a clock.

Imagine the model of galactic time, where all the star systems are in the same now. It is the same time throughout all the galaxy. You may have heard of galactic time before. Do the words: "Captain's Log . . . Star Date: 28 point 53 point 6" mean anything to you?

"Now" is to find your art. To understand time is to create your art.

Timing

To paraphrase Shakespeare, all the world is a stage and each being plays many roles. I would like to add three things to this. One, props and costumes are very important. Two, each individual writes his or her own script, so write a leading role. Bit parts can become boring. Three, timing is everything. A role and a game are one and the same.

Timing . . . if something is not yet to happen, then no amount of will can get it to happen. In fact, attempting something whose time has not come is called "willful behavior." This concept is mentioned in the section on "effortlessness," page 41.

If we are laboring to complete a project and the timing is off, notice your attention span. When you observe fatigue setting in, create a break. It serves us far better if you do not choose to become fried. This is compassion for self. It's all in the timing. The other word for diplomacy is timing.

Authority

Authority = Knowing. The word respect means literally to look again. Dissing respect (disrespect) is the refusal to look again. Let us look again at authority. There were two reasons we respected someone. One was fear, the other is love. We pretend to acknowledge someone as an authority figure out of fear. We respect someone because we love them.

In the great age of information it may be impossible to be an authority on everything. In order to function as a group, we have agreed to delegate authority. This functioning, this co-creation, looks like acknowledging another's knowing on a particular subject. This is co-creating authority.

The idea is to know our place in relationship to authority, not to give away our power to it. Our relationship with it is a love relationship. We love someone in that he or she got the education to be an authority on some subject. Therefore, we can have the benefit from the knowledge, without having had to go read all those books, etc.

Captain Picard is beloved, for he agreed to play the role model: "Human being who, under no circumstances chooses to give up personal power." When Picard was tortured by the Cardasians, when he was turned into a Borg, when everyone lost their identity, he did not give up his power.

In defying authority, we give away our power to it. To defy another's authority is the fear that we don't own our own authority. To make someone wrong in turn makes us wrong. We used to arm ourselves and go to war with anyone who disagreed. We were so addicted to being right. Any argument was based on a fear that we didn't have authority.

As soon as we defy authority, we acknowledge it as a greater authority than our own. As we are all self-governing, there is no requirement for being governed externally, and no use in defying authority.

When life looks like constant scrapes with authority figures, it is because we don't own our own authority. Therefore it is created externally.

The physical body has a back-up system for the authority lesson. It is the neck! The number of rings in the flesh of the throat represent the number of past lives where we have defied authority and then been beheaded or hung. Choose to get the authority lesson and these rings go away.

Have you ever called someone a pain in the neck? You were referring to an authority figure who was attempting to offer you a remembering. Apparently, you were defying them or you wouldn't have been in pain. PAIN = FEAR. To defy someone's authority creates them as an authority.

Owning your power harms no one. We are all quite equal. We are all a part of God, not apart from God.

The left hand of our author.

I am my own Authority Figure. I acknowledge other authority figures. We all share authority. Authority is in owning knowing. Physically, we own it in our bodies, we know it by heart, and it is displayed in eye contact. It doesn't have anything to do with the college degree that graces the wall, or the uniforms we wear. Notice that it may be impossible to look someone in the eye if we do not believe in ourselves.

The word "author" is obviously short for "authority." As the one who agreed to play the role of an author, I own that I am an authority on speaking and writing English. Thank you for co-creating me owning such authority, by reading this book. Feedback is quite welcome.

I could hang any number of degrees after my name. I've been ordained three times. At one time I thought of putting the entire alphabet after my name (well, at least the vowels). Because I speak English. How about putting your own initials after your name? You are the greatest authority on yourself.

We are all equals. We all hold a Ph.D. in many areas. When I am with my peers, we allow each other to be the authority on particular subjects. Everyone brings their "own" stories to the campfire. Thank you for allowing me to bring this book to your fire.

Command = Creation Permission = Co-creation Permission to Give Commands

Under some circumstances, it is appropriate that you ask for permission. Certainly, I would ask for permission before entering the King's Chamber of the Great Pyramid in Egypt. Or anyone's sacred space, for that matter. It is protocol, a ceremonial negotiation, and it is essential.

Every time you move your body, you command. You are all God in your individual universe. As your ownership of your personal power matures, it becomes possible to command the ethers. Human beings are allowed to give commands. By your own power. Command and permission balance each other. Permission means "per our mission." Command means "God together with man or woman."

After consciously feeling the Love of Earth (permission), stand on her barefoot. Command your body to connect with the mother. Feel the energy come up through the legs. Build it in a ball in the kundalini chakra. Then move the ball up to the heart chakra.

Feel the love of the father (permission) coming through your crown chakra. Feel it in the heart. Then raise your arms and command your body to connect to the father universe. Command the universe that you are healed. "Feel the Flow!"

But, wait! What if I should be unable to finish this book? I think I need to try. What of the karma? Oh never mind, it's probably just my imagination. Or maybe it was just my luck. I'm gonna go modulate my frequency and tune in on a different channel. Love us all!

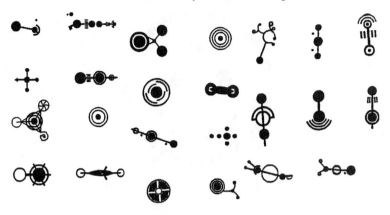

These are Crop Circles. One does not have to know them. One does not have to study them. Just look at them and they activate the new DNA.

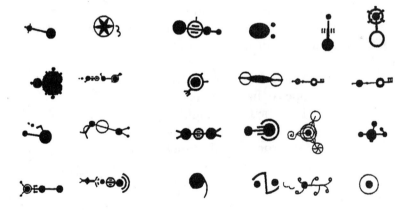

HAVE A NICE INCARNATION

The End

The end? There is no such thing. Therefore beginnings don't exist either. The thoughts of beginnings and endings are yet again myths. They have made our reality very choppy. To no longer perceive reality made up of beginnings and endings frees us. If we stop using the concept of beginnings and endings, then we all live together as the ocean instead of the individual drops.

> Shape Shift for Success
> Speak the Language of Light,
> Live the Life of Light.
> I love you beyond imagination.
> And through all remembering

R. Neville Johnston

Our History is not our destiny.
*Consciously own
the power from speech!
Blessings on us All.*

Index

EMANCIPATION PROCLAMATION

From this day forward, and made official by this document,

_____ is declared free of all forms of slavery, bondage, indenture, restraint, curse, spell, guilt, or hinderance in any form; from this or any other lifetime. And further, this entity is made *sui juris*, in full control of his or her free will and creating 100 percent of his or her life.

Resident Authority by: _____ Date _____

Signed and agreed by: _____ Date _____

Witnessed by: _____ Date _____

cut here